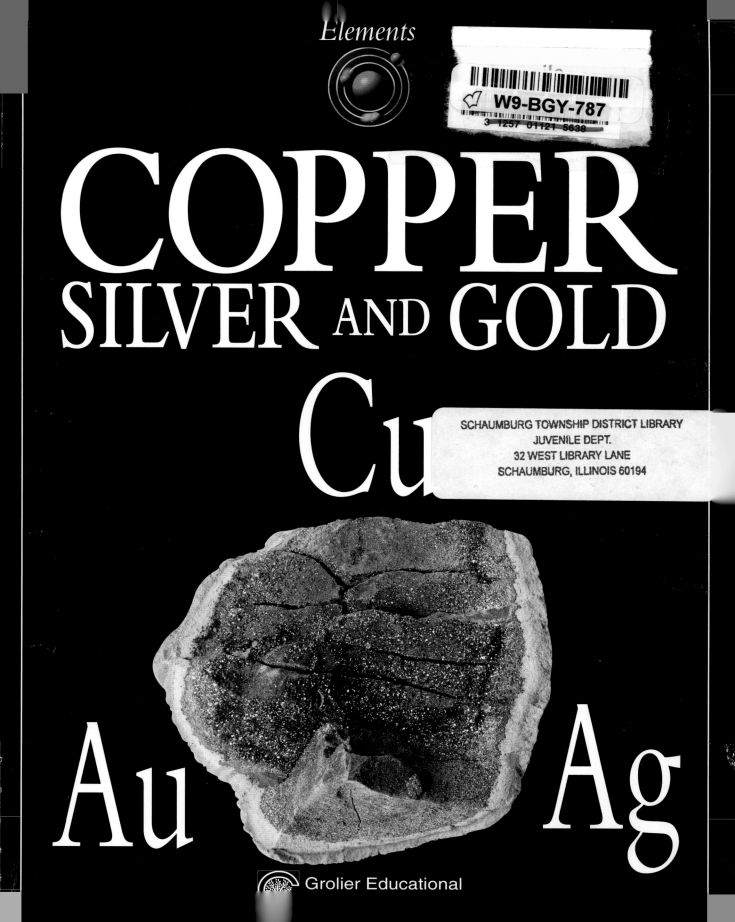

COPPER
SILVER AND GOLD

Cu

Au

Ag

Grolier Educational

How to use this book

This book has been carefully developed to help you understand the chemistry of the elements. In it you will find a systematic and comprehensive coverage of the basic qualities of each element. Each two-page entry contains information at various levels of technical content and language, along with definitions of useful technical terms, as shown in the thumbnail diagram to the right. There is a comprehensive glossary of technical terms at the back of the book, along with an extensive index, key facts, an explanation of the periodic table, and a description of how to interpret chemical equations.

The main text follows the sequence of information in the book and summarizes the concepts presented on the two pages.

Technical definitions.

Substatements flesh out the ideas in the main text with more fact and specific explanation.

Equations are written as symbols and sometimes given as "ball-and-stick" diagrams – see page 48.

Photographs and diagrams have been carefully selected and annotated for clarity.

Also... explains advanced concepts.

Author
Brian Knapp, BSc, PhD
Project consultant
Keith B. Walshaw, MA, BSc, DPhil
(Head of Chemistry, Leighton Park School)
Industrial consultant
Jack Brettle, BSc, PhD (Chief Research Scientist, Pilkington plc)
Art Director
Duncan McCrae, BSc
Editor
Elizabeth Walker, BA
Special photography
Ian Gledhill
Illustrations
David Woodroffe
Electronic page makeup
Julie James Graphic Design
Designed and produced by
EARTHSCAPE EDITIONS
Print consultants
Landmark Production Consultants Ltd
Reproduced by
Leo Reprographics
Printed and bound by
Paramount Printing Company Ltd, Hong Kong

First published in the United States in 1996 by Grolier Educational, Sherman Turnpike, Danbury, CT 06816

First reprinted in 1997

Copyright © 1996
Atlantic Europe Publishing Company Limited

Cataloging information may be obtained directly from Grolier Educational.

Set ISBN 0–7172–7572–8
Volume ISBN 0–7172–7577–9
Library of Congress Number: 95–082222

Acknowledgments
The publishers would like to thank the following for their kind help and advice: *The Copper Development Association, Jonathan Frankel of J. M. Frankel and Associates, Ian and Catherine Gledhill of Shutters, Dr Angus W. R. McCrae, Rolls-Royce plc and Charles Schotman.*

Picture credits
All photographs are from the **Earthscape Editions** photolibrary except the following:
(c=center t=top b=bottom l=left =right)
Copper Development Association 11br, 12; **Ian Gledhill** 32bc; courtesy of **Rolls-Royce plc** FRONT COVER, 16/17; by permission of **The Syndics of Cambridge University Library** 37t, 37b, 39b and **ZEFA** 10b, 38c.

Front cover: Copper is used for the core of this huge generator in a power station.
Title page: A spectacular sample of chalcopyrite ore.

This product is manufactured from sustainable managed forests. For every tree cut down at least one more is planted.

The demonstrations described or illustrated in this book are not for replication. The Publisher cannot accept any responsibility for any accidents or injuries that may result from conducting the experiments described or illustrated in this book.

Contents

Introduction

An element is a substance that cannot be broken down into a simpler substance by any known means. Each of the 92 naturally occurring elements is therefore one of the fundamental materials from which everything in the Universe is made. This book is about copper, silver and gold.

These three elements are often called the "coinage metals" because they are used to make most of the world's coins. One reason for this is that none of the coinage metals is very reactive with other elements, and therefore they are very resistant to corrosion.

Copper

Copper, a soft orangy-colored metal, was one of the first metals to be used in the ancient world. It has been exploited for at least 7,000 years. Its name comes from the Latin, *cuprum*, which means "metal of Cyprus," an island in the Mediterranean Sea where the Romans had large copper mines.

Copper is an excellent conductor of heat and electricity, and is found in most of the flexible cables used in the world. Its softness also makes it suitable for tubing for water pipes and central heating systems, because it can be soldered easily and readily bent to fit around corners. Above all, it can be mixed with other metals to make extremely useful alloys such as brass and bronze.

▼ New York's Statue of Liberty has a pleasing green patina, but the copper is otherwise little affected even after a century of exposure to the weather.

Silver

Silver is a white, shiny heavy metal. Its symbol is Ag, after *argentum*, a Latin word meaning "white and shining." Silver has been sought after since the earliest times and is regarded as a precious metal, just as gems are precious stones. Yet although silver is known for its precious value, only 16% of all the silver used in the world is used for coins and jewelry, while 40% goes to make photographic film. Much of the rest is used in industry and health services. Mirrors, for example, are mostly made by silvering the back of glass.

Gold

The chemical symbol for gold is Au, after the Latin word for gold, *aurum*. Gold is one of the rarest elements found on Earth and has been sought by people since ancient times. One of the reasons for this is that it is a soft metal that nearly always occurs in pure, or native, form. Ancient peoples could thus make use of gold along with silver and copper without special tools and without refining.

Most of the world's gold is in sea water, where it is too dispersed to be collected. On land it is found in veins and in small fragments in river beds and coastal sands. Its discovery has set off many gold rushes throughout the world.

Gold resists corrosion better than almost any other material. It does not tarnish but remains a bright, lustrous, deep yellow color indefinitely. In fact this resistance to corrosion has made the metal vital in the electronics industry, where it is used, for example, to make electrical contacts.

▶ An untarnished one-cent coin. Most copper-colored coins are made from an alloy of copper, tin and zinc. Many of the silver-colored coins we use today are an alloy of copper and nickel.

Copper ores

Copper is a metal that was deposited from hot sulfur solutions, created as volcanoes were erupting. The hot solutions concentrated the copper by up to a thousand times more than would be normally found in rocks. The resultant enriched rocks are called copper ores.

As the hot fluid made its way from magma chambers through cracks and fissures in the rocks, copper ores were deposited in narrow veins.

The island of Cyprus in the Mediterranean Sea is one such ancient volcanic area. The ancient Romans mined the ore there.

The Romans only mined deposits of native copper, that is, copper metal that is not bound up in any compound. This pure form of copper was very easy to work and did not need refining. However, most copper occurs as compounds, especially as sulfides; and because they need to be refined, they have only begun to be used relatively recently.

▲ A piece of chrysocolla.

Chrysocolla

Copper silicate and copper carbonate have a characteristic green color. Compare this picture to the copper carbonate patina on the Statue of Liberty on page 4. The mineral shown here is called chrysocolla, a copper aluminum silicate.

Chalcopyrite and bornite

Chalcopyrite and bornite are minerals containing both copper and iron sulfides. They are the source of half of the world's copper ores.

Chalcopyrite is a brassy-colored mineral, while bornite is often a rich peacock-blue (in fact it is often called peacock ore). They were formed during intense volcanic activity, when hot liquids were pushed through fissures in the rocks, cooling and solidifying to yield minerals with a high metal content. Silver and gold were formed in much the same way, and for this reason the coinage metals are often mined together.

The sample shown here is made mainly of bornite, but if you look closely you will see the gold speckles of chalcopyrite as well.

▶ A piece of bornite or peacock ore with speckles of chalcopyrite.

► A piece of native copper.

magma: the molten rock that forms a balloon-shaped chamber in the rock below a volcano. It is fed by rock moving upward from below the crust.

native metal: a pure form of a metal, not combined as a compound. Native metal is more common in poorly reactive elements than in those that are very reactive.

ore: a rock containing enough of a useful substance to make mining it worthwhile.

refining: the separation of a mixture into the simpler substances of which it is made. In the case of a rock, it means the extraction of the metal that is mixed up in the rock.

silicate: a compound containing silicon and oxygen (known as silica).

sulfide: a sulfur compound that contains no oxygen.

vein: a mineral deposit different from, and usually cutting across, the surrounding rocks. Most mineral and metal-bearing veins are deposits filling fractures.

Native copper

Copper is not a very reactive element. Thus, like silver and gold, which are also slow to react chemically, it is sometimes found in pure form. A natural occurrence of pure copper is called native copper. The shape reflects the deep underground fissures in which it was originally deposited and is known as a dendritic pattern.

The largest piece of native copper ever found was in Minesota Mine, Michigan. It weighed over 520 tons.

◄ This is banded malachite, a copper carbonate and a useful ore.

Reducing copper oxide

Copper is mainly found in the form of a black ore, copper oxide, or a brassy-colored ore, copper sulfide. In both cases the metal has to be separated from its compound.

The demonstration on this page shows how copper can be extracted from its compound. The ore is copper oxide, a compound of copper and oxygen. To obtain pure copper the oxygen has to be removed, using a process called reduction.

The reducing agent used here is carbon monoxide gas, which is colorless but inflammable. The reaction produces carbon dioxide gas, which is also colorless but does not burn. So the key to watching this sequence is to look for where the flame appears and disappears. In this way you can tell which gas is in the tube!

❶▼ The black copper oxide is placed in a special glass tube with a small hole near the rounded end. At the start, the tube is full of air. This is swept away by pumping in carbon monoxide gas.

The black copper oxide is heated with a Bunsen burner.

Carbon monoxide gas is passed in through this tube.

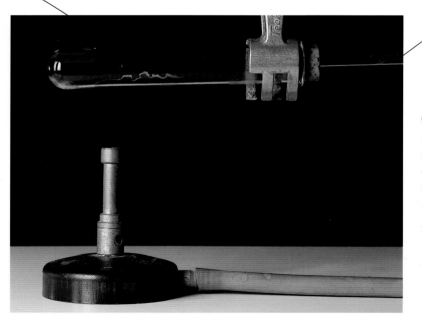

❷◄ The copper oxide continues to be reduced, and the oxygen combines with the carbon monoxide to form carbon dioxide. Carbon dioxide does not ignite, so the flame goes out.

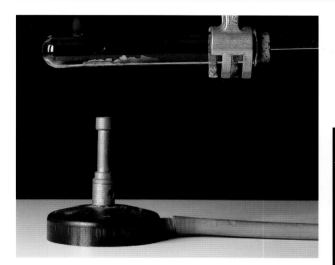

oxide: a compound that includes oxygen and one other element.

reduction: the removal of oxygen from a substance.

Closeup of the end of the tube showing the carbon monoxide gas burning with a blue flame.

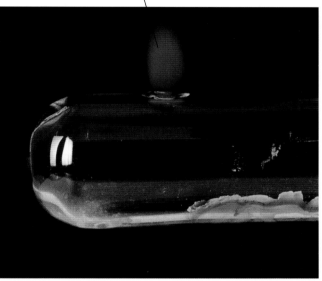

❸▲▶ Reactions between elements and compounds are often very slow at room temperature. To speed up the rate of reaction, the copper oxide is heated using the flame from a Bunsen burner.

The blue flame coming from the small hole in the tube is produced by burning carbon monoxide gas. Notice that the copper oxide is glowing orange on the surface, which shows that the oxygen has been removed.

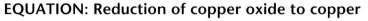

❹▲ Eventually all of the oxygen is removed from the copper oxide powder, and only copper is left.

EQUATION: Reduction of copper oxide to copper

Copper oxide + carbon monoxide ⇨ copper + carbon dioxide

$$CuO(s) \quad + \quad CO(g) \quad ⇨ \quad Cu(s) \quad + \quad CO_2(g)$$

Copper

Oxygen

Carbon

9

Mining and smelting copper ores

About nine-tenths of the world's reserves of copper are found in just four areas: the great Basin of the western United States, central Canada, the Andes regions of Peru and Chile, and Zambia. In each case the extraction of copper is of crucial importance to the country. In the case of Zambia the reserves are the mainstay of the country's economy, with a chain of major cities making up the "Copper Belt." The largest deposit of copper in the world is at Chuquicamata, Chile; but the largest refiner of copper is the United States, which also boasts the world's largest copper mine, in Utah.

The amount of copper in the ground is relatively small, and most of it occurs in low-grade ores that have to be processed twice to extract the copper. This is why it is important to reuse as much copper as possible, and why about one-third of copper consumed in most industrial countries is recycled from scrap.

Mining

Over 90% of the world's copper ore is obtained by strip mining in vast open-cut mines. Large blast holes are drilled in the ore, the material is blasted loose, and it is then put into dump trucks and taken to the enriching plant.

▶ Copper ores can be mined with as little as about one-half of 1% copper content. This picture, from Arizona, shows one of the world's most important copper mines.

The total world reserve of copper is just over 200 million metric tons. It will provide enough copper to last about 50 years.

Concentration

Most ore contains only about 1% metal, so the ore must be concentrated before it is sent for smelting and refining. This is done by first pulverizing the ore, then separating it by flotation, and finally drying it. At the end of this process the metal-to-ore ratio is about one to three.

The ore-flotation method

The flotation method is a way of separating ore mineral from gangue (rock that contains no metal), thus enriching the ore before final processing.

gangue: the unwanted material in an ore.

The ores to be enriched are first ground to a fine grit, which still contains particles of copper mixed up with gangue. To separate the copper particles from the gangue, the grit is introduced to a bath of water containing a foaming agent, which produces a kind of bubble bath combined with a special oil-based chemical that makes the copper particles water-repellent.

When jets of air are forced up through the bath, the water-repellent copper particles are picked up by the bubbles of foam and float to the surface, making a froth. The froth is skimmed off the surface, and the enriched ore is taken away for refining.

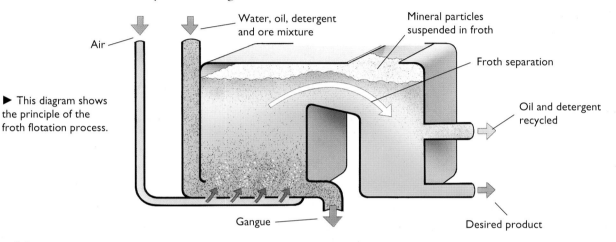

Air

Water, oil, detergent and ore mixture

Mineral particles suspended in froth

Froth separation

Oil and detergent recycled

Gangue

Desired product

► This diagram shows the principle of the froth flotation process.

Smelting

Most copper ores are difficult to refine, although smelting removes most of the impurities from the enriched ore. The easiest ores to smelt are the copper oxides. Carbon monoxide gas needed to reduce the ore is produced by heating coke, a source of carbon, and feeding in a jet of air. This carbon and oxygen from the air react to form carbon monoxide, which reduces the copper oxide to copper. The copper can then be tapped from the base of the furnace.

Copper sulfides present greater difficulties. The copper is removed by heating and the process may require the introduction of oxygen. At the same time, the sulfur is oxidized to sulfur dioxide gas. Since sulfur dioxide is one of the major contributors to acid rain, many modern factories recover as much of the gas as possible to be used in the production of sulfuric acid.

▲ Molten copper being cast into ingots for later use. A continuously rotating wheel is used for this process.

EQUATION: Reduction of copper ore containing both oxides and sulfides by heating

Copper sulfide + copper oxide ➪ copper + sulfur dioxide

$$CuS(s) + 2CuO(s) \Rightarrow 3Cu(s) + SO_2(g)$$

Electrical refining of copper

Even the best of chemical reactions cannot completely remove all of the impurities in a metal, so ores refined in a furnace do not produce pure metals. This is why many metals are refined to their final stage of purity by electrical means in a process called electrolysis.

Impure copper from the furnace is used as one of the electrodes of an electrolysis cell. The other electrode is made from a thin sheet of pure copper. The copper is then refined by placing the two electrodes in a copper sulfate bath and passing a current between them. The impure copper on the anode corrodes, and copper ions pass through the electrolyte, collecting on the cathode sheet as pure copper.

When the cathode has acquired a sufficient thickness of pure copper, it is lifted from the electrolysis cell and replaced with a new electrode. Similarly, when the anode has corroded completely away, it is replaced with a new ingot of smelted metal. The cathodes are then melted down and made into wire and sheet metal.

The laboratory demonstration of electrolysis and the giant industrial equivalent are shown on these pages.

▶ Copper cathodes, heavily plated with copper, are lifted from the electrolytic cells.

Laboratory electrolysis

A demonstration of electrolysis can be done using a beaker and two copper strips. A dry battery serves as the source of electrical current. The electrolyte is reagent quality copper sulfate solution.

Signs of corrosion and plating are evident within minutes, and a completely corroded strip can be produced within a day or so.

electrolysis: an electrical-chemical process that uses an electric current to cause the breakup of a compound and the movement of metal ions in a solution. The process happens in many natural situations (as for example in rusting) and is also commonly used in industry for purifying (refining) metals or for plating metal objects with a fine, even metal coating.

electrolyte: a solution that conducts electricity.

slag: a mixture of substances that are waste products of a furnace.

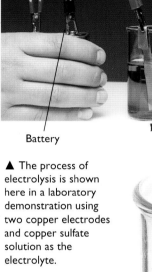

Battery

▲ The process of electrolysis is shown here in a laboratory demonstration using two copper electrodes and copper sulfate solution as the electrolyte.

Pure copper deposited on the cathode

Copper sulfate solution

Anode

Also...

In the process of refining copper by electrolysis, several rare metals such as silver and gold are also obtained from the ore. The recovery of these helps to pay the huge cost of electrical energy used to refine copper.

▶ After a few hours the anode has corroded during electrolysis. By contrast, the cathode has been plated with pure copper.

Cathode on which the metal is deposited

Copper as a metal

About nine million tons of copper are used every year in a wide variety of ways. About half of all copper is used in the electrical industry (see next page). Copper is also used for water pipes, roofing, locks and hinges, coins, and vehicle radiators.

Many of these uses have come about because, of all the common metals, copper is outstanding in its resistance to attack by oxygen and water. Copper only changes to copper oxide when the temperature reaches 300°C. It is not corroded by water or steam, which is why it can be used for hot and cold water systems and central heating and air-conditioning systems. It is not even affected by most dilute acids, although concentrated nitric acid reacts violently with copper, as shown below.

▲ Heated copper compounds produce a characteristic blue flame.

◄◄ The picture on the far left shows fuming concentrated nitric acid being poured on to copper turnings (finely divided copper that provides a large surface area for fast reaction). The picture on the near left shows the resulting reaction. The copper is transformed into blue copper nitrate and large amounts of nitrogen dioxide are given off.

EQUATION: Copper and fuming nitric acid

Copper turnings + fuming nitric acid ⇨ copper nitrate + water + nitrogen dioxide

$$Cu(s) + 4HNO_3(l) \Rightarrow Cu(NO_3)_2(s) + 2H_2O(l) + 2NO_2(g)$$

blue

The reactivity of copper

Metals can be arranged in a list, with the most reactive at the top and the least reactive at the bottom. Many metals are subject to corrosion when placed in damp air or damp soil. The most vulnerable of all are the most reactive elements.

Copper comes near the bottom of the reactivity series because it is only slightly reactive. This low reactivity means that copper objects can be placed out in exposed locations without fear that they will corrode away.

corrosion: the *slow* decay of a substance resulting from contact with gases and liquids in the environment. The term is often applied to metals.

REACTIVITY SERIES	
Element	Reactivity
potassium	*most reactive*
sodium	
calcium	
magnesium	
aluminum	
manganese	
chromium	
zinc	
iron	
cadmium	
tin	
lead	
copper	
mercury	
silver	
gold	
platinum	*least reactive*

► Copper is a good conductor of heat. This makes for efficient use of energy and precise control of the cooking temperature when copper is used for cooking implements such as this jam-making pan.

◄ Copper is widely used for decorative metalware, either as pure copper or as an alloy such as brass.

▲ Copper is used for water-carrying pipework because water will not corrode it.

Copper as a conductor

All metals have the ability to transfer, or conduct, heat and electricity; however, copper is among the most efficient at conducting both.

An electric current is simply a flow of electrons. Metals can conduct electricity because they are made up of a "honeycomb" (known as a lattice) of positively charged ions in a "sea" of electrons. In the case of copper, these electrons are not bound to any one copper ion but can move freely. This is what makes copper such a good conductor of electricity.

When heat is applied to copper, the atoms of the metal vibrate and pass energy across the honeycomb. Copper conducts heat better than most metals because of the arrangement of its atoms.

▼ This diagram shows how the tiny electrons in the copper wiring are free to move easily in the honeycomb framework provided by the copper atoms.

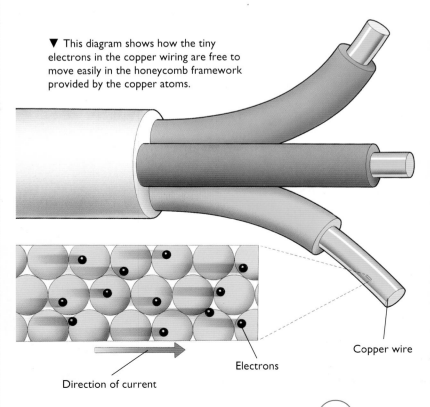

Copper wire

Electrons

Direction of current

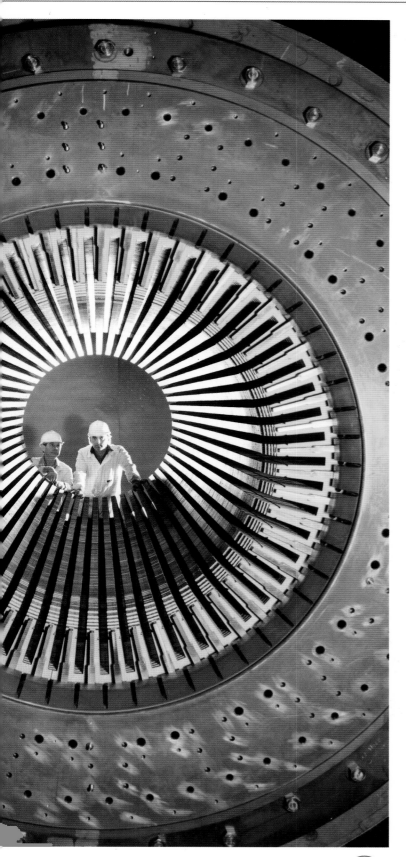

electron: a tiny, negatively charged particle that is part of an atom. The flow of electrons through a solid material such as a wire produces an electric current.

ion: an atom, or group of atoms, that has gained or lost one or more electrons and so developed an electrical charge.

◀ Looking through the inside of a large electrical motor. The copper wire carries the electrical current that generates the magnetic field that, in turn, causes the drive shaft of the motor to turn.

Copper in printed circuits

A printed circuit is made from a rigid baseboard of insulating material with conductors stuck to its surfaces. To make a printed circuit, a sheet of copper foil is stuck to both sides of the baseboard. The copper foil is then sprayed with a film of light-sensitive (silver-based) material. A mask is made up of the connections that are required, and placed on the film. The film is then exposed to light and the board put into a photographic developer, which removes all undeveloped parts of the film.

Next the board is placed in an acid solution that dissolves away all parts of the copper not protected by the developed film. This leaves behind the pattern of connections on the board, ready for the electrical components to be added.

▼ A printed circuit board showing the conducting circuit of fine copper connecting the wide variety of electronic devices.

Copper alloys: brass

An alloy is a mixture of metals. Copper forms alloys more easily than most other metals. Each of the alloying metals gives the alloy its own special properties. Some metals make the alloy stronger, others change its color, make it easier to machine or make it even more resistant to corrosion or wear. The metals most often alloyed with copper are shown on the next few pages.

Brass

Brass is one of the most widely used alloys. It is mainly copper alloyed with between 5 and 40% zinc. Brass is often used for corrosion-resistant decorative purposes such as door hardware. It is much harder and stronger than copper and it will machine well.

The most common mixture of brass contains 36% zinc and is known as common brass. The properties of brass can be altered significantly by adding small quantities of other elements. Those most commonly used are lead, tin, aluminum, manganese, iron, nickel, arsenic and silicon. For example, by adding up to 3% lead, the machinability of brass can be improved significantly.

Copper-rich brasses have special uses, such as making the percussion caps of ammunition; those with between 10 and 20% zinc are called gilding metals and are used for decorative brasswork and jewelry. This form of brass will take an enamel well and is easy to braze.

As the amount of zinc is increased still further, the brass develops the property of being easily shaped when hot. This material is used to make inexpensive but complex engineering shapes that are easy to machine.

However, even higher proportions of zinc make the alloy more susceptible to corrosion when the brass is placed in water. To counteract this problem, arsenic is added to the alloy.

Tin can also be added to brass to improve its corrosion resistance; and tin-zinc-copper brasses, in which there is 1% tin, are known as admiralty brass because of their suitability for use on ships.

▼▶ Brass is usually made from about 64% copper and 36% zinc. Adjusting the proportions produces very different properties; for example, the alloy becomes harder as more zinc is added. Other metals can be added to give additional qualities, as the diagram on the right illustrates.

Copper

Zinc

▼ A jug made of brass and copper.

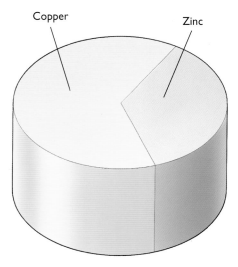

Brass top and handle. The tarnished surface has been cleaned using a solvent.

This part of the jug is made of copper.

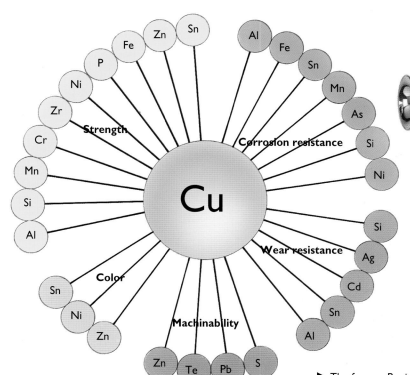

Strength: Al, Si, Mn, Cr, Zr, Ni, P, Fe, Zn, Sn

Corrosion resistance: Al, Fe, Sn, Mn, As, Si, Ni

Wear resistance: Si, Ag, Cd, Sn, Al

Machinability: Zn, Te, Pb, S

Color: Sn, Ni, Zn

Cu

▲ Brass is commonly used for musical instruments because it is relatively light, easy to shape, strong even when thin and has an attractive color.

Decorative brass has a low zinc content (usually between 10 and 20%). It is called architectural brass.

Tarnished surface from exposure to air (see page 28)

▶ The famous Benin bronzes from southern Nigeria are highly regarded pieces of art, the earliest of which were made 700 years ago. Most Benin bronzes are however made of alloys that contain more zinc than tin and so are really brass. Their intricate shapes are cast using the lost-wax process.

Shape-changing brass

A form of brass can be made that changes its shape above a certain temperature and returns to its original shape when it cools down. This "memory" brass can be used to operate safety devices and other applications. It is used, for example, in the automatic switching devices in many electric jugs and kettles.

Copper alloys: bronze

Bronze is an alloy of copper that is significantly different from brass. Bronze is a copper alloy with tin as its major secondary constituent (brass is an alloy with zinc, as described on page 18).

Bronze has been used since ancient times for decorative metal objects and also for coins. It was one of the earliest metal alloys used, giving rise to the first metalworking age, known as the Bronze Age, over 3,000 years ago. Bronze Age people, however, did not know about alloying (mixing) metals but used copper ores that naturally contained tin impurities.

▲▼ Bronze is usually made from about 78% copper and 12% tin. The less tin, the softer the metal will be. Usually no more than 25% tin is added.

Adding zinc and lead to the bronze alloy produces a material that is much more suitable for casting.

An alloy with about nine-tenths copper and equal proportions of the other metals is called gunmetal. It was commonly used in cannons, not only for its corrosion resistance but also for its machinability. Above is a cannon that was used at Gettysburg during the American Civil War.

Wrought bronze

Wrought bronze, also known as phosphor bronze, has a low tin content (perhaps 8% or less) and one-third of a percent phosphorus. It is commonly used for bearings in machines or engines where shafts continually rotate. It is also used for coins.

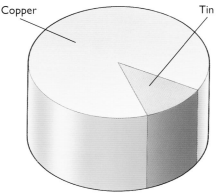

◄ A bronze coin with portrait of the Roman emperor Hadrian who reigned between 117 and 138 A.D. This particular coin was minted sometime between 126 and 138 A.D. Despite being in damp soil for more than 1,850 years, the coin still shows a lot of detail from the original casting.

Gastight or porous bronzes

If lead is used in bronze alloys, the alloy will run into any pores created as the molten alloy sets. Leaded bronze is thus gastight and can be used for pressure vessels.

On the other hand, bronze can be made intentionally porous so that it can be used as a filter. For this purpose tin and copper powders are mixed, then heated in the absence of air. The result is a porous bronze.

Bell-making bronze

There is a wide range of specialized bronzes, each one having its own distinctive properties. Up to 12% tin is normally used in making a bronze, but up to 20% is used for bell-making bronze, which is little used for engineering. The brittleness of bell-making bronze makes the bells liable to crack. However, this disadvantage is outweighed by the particularly rich tones made by the metal.

▼ The famous Liberty Bell is kept in Philadelphia, Pennsylvania. Bell metals like that used for the Liberty Bell contain about 20–25% tin and are very hard, giving them the appropriate resonance. However, this also makes them very brittle. The crack in the Liberty Bell is so bad that it cannot be rung.

porous: a material containing many small holes or cracks. Quite often the pores are connected, and liquids, such as water or oil, can move through them.

▼ An English bronze bell foundry at work in the 18th century. The furnace can be seen in the background. The molten bronze was poured into a mold and allowed to solidify before being taken out and filed to shape and tune the bell.

Corrosion resistance

Silicon bronze is used in places where there is a great danger of corrosion, such as in a chemical plant. This alloy contains up to 3% silicon. Bronzes made of alloys of aluminum and copper have similar properties.

▲ The Chinese, Romans and Greeks used bronze extensively for casting sculptures, and it is still used for this purpose today, as shown by the Bucking Bronco statue from Denver, Colorado, above. However, bronze is now considered expensive and labour intensive to use in comparison with other alloys and metals available.

Copper in the environment

Both plants and animals need a certain amount of copper as part of their diets. In animals, copper is used in the body to help release energy and is usually found in protein. It is required as a micronutrient, that is, it is vital but is only needed in very small amounts. Too little or too much can be dangerous. Copper is a natural part of most soils and is used by plants too as a micronutrient to aid growth.

▲ Where the copper content of a soil is low, plants can suffer from poor growth and become much more prone to disease. The different rates of growth from different amounts of copper can be seen in this picture. The wheat on the left has an adequate amount of copper; the one on the right is copper-deficient.

▼ Copper-based fungicide is commonly sprayed on fruit trees.

Copper in gardens and farms

The main copper-based fertilizer is copper sulfate, which can be applied to the soil or to the leaves of growing plants as a spray.

Plants are able to benefit from a spray of copper, but many pests are not. Both copper nitrate and copper sulfate poison fungi (molds), algae and bacteria. For this reason copper salts are used extensively by farmers and gardeners.

Copper sulfate has traditionally been used to make a fungicide called Bordeaux mixture, once used on the vineyards of the Bordeaux region of France. Seeds are also dipped in copper sulfate solution to prevent disease.

micronutrient: an element that the body requires in small amounts. Another term is trace element.

protein: molecules that help build tissue and bone and therefore make new body cells. Proteins contain amino acids.

Copper and pollution

Copper tailings, the waste products of copper mines, contain high concentrations of copper. At these levels they are poisonous to plants, and waste heaps remain bare of vegetation. Care has to be taken to make sure contaminated water does not reach nearby rivers.

◀ This building is being sprayed with a copper-based fungicide during construction to help protect it against attack by mold.

Copper compounds as preservatives

In the home and on exposed timber such as fences, copper salts can be used to prevent mold growing in damp areas. Copper sulfate is routinely added to wallpaper paste for this purpose.

▲ Fenceposts and other wood intended for prolonged outdoor use is pressure-treated with copper and other compounds to prevent rotting.

Copper sulfate

One of the best known compounds of copper is copper sulfate (formerly known as blue vitriol because of its deep blue color). It is prepared by reacting copper oxide or copper carbonate with warm, dilute sulfuric acid. The solution then turns a translucent blue.

To make copper sulfate crystals, the solution is evaporated until it is saturated (it can hold no more copper sulfate in solution). Large crystals of copper sulfate can be grown in this solution by suspending a small "seed" crystal in the saturated solution, around which larger crystals will form. Smaller crystals are produced by evaporating the solution to a small volume. Each technique is shown in the pictures on this page.

❶◀ Dilute sulfuric acid is poured on to (black) copper oxide

❷▶ The reaction occurs as the reagents are stirred.

EQUATION: Producing copper sulfate

Copper oxide + dilute sulfuric acid ⇨ copper sulfate + water

$$CuO(s) \quad + \quad H_2SO_4(aq) \quad ⇨ \quad CuSO_4(aq) \quad + \quad H_2O(l)$$

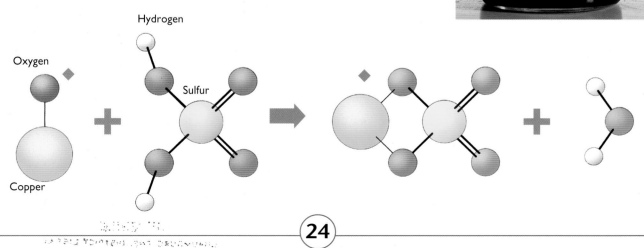

Hydrogen

Oxygen

Sulfur

Copper

❸◀ The solution soon clears and becomes bright blue. This is copper sulfate dissolved in water.

anhydrous: a term meaning that water has been removed by heating. Many hydrated salts are crystalline. When they are heated and the water is driven off, the material changes to an anhydrous powder.

hydrate: a solid compound in crystalline form that contains molecular water. Hydrates commonly form when a solution of a soluble salt is evaporated. The water that forms part of a hydrate crystal is known as the "water of crystallization." It can usually be removed by heating, leaving an anhydrous salt.

reagent: a starting material for a reaction.

◀▼ Copper sulfate crystals like these of varying size can be grown from a saturated copper sulfate solution.

▲▶ Crystals of hydrated copper sulfate (above) are deep blue. However, when the water is driven off, the substance changes to a very light blue powder, called anhydrous copper sulfate (right).

Copper colors

A characteristic of many metals is that their compounds produce a variety of colored substances, usually quite unlike the color of the metals in their native state.

Copper forms several such compounds. For example, copper oxide is black; copper carbonate is green; copper sulfate and copper nitrate are blue. Copper sulfide may be black or, if it is an ore, brassy yellow, depending on the amount of iron it contains.

Some examples of these colors are shown on this page, but other examples can be found on page 6.

❶▲ Nitric acid is being poured onto black copper oxide.

EQUATION: Producing copper nitrate

Copper oxide + nitric acid ⇨ copper nitrate + water

$$CuO(s) + 2HNO_3(l) ⇨ Cu(NO_3)_2(s) + H_2O(l)$$

❷▼ Crystals of copper nitrate form. They are a brighter blue than copper sulfate.

Nitrogen

Oxygen

▶ This represents copper nitrate.

Copper

▼ Pure copper is an orangy color, as shown by these coppered nails.

Green copper coating

Copper corrodes in moist air due to the combined effects of copper, water, oxygen and carbon dioxide from the air.

This makes a pleasing green copper carbonate coating known as a patina, or incrustation. A patina protects the surface of a substance from further attack and forms on both copper, brass and bronze objects.

gelatinous: a term meaning made with water. Because a gelatinous precipitate is mostly water, it is of a similar density to water and will float or lie suspended in the liquid.

patina: a surface coating that develops on metals and protects them from further corrosion.

EQUATION: How copper develops a green color when exposed to the environment

Copper + carbon dioxide + oxygen (dissolved in water) ➪ copper carbonate

$$2Cu(s) + 2CO_2(g) + O_2(aq) \; ➪ \; 2CuCO_3(s)$$

◀ The Statue of Liberty has a green copper carbonate coating.

▶ **Preparing blue copper hydroxide**
Blue copper hydroxide gelatinous solid is formed by reaction of a copper sulfate solution with a sodium hydroxide solution.

This precipitate shows where the drop of sodium hydroxide solution has reacted with the copper sulfate to produce a blob of copper hydroxide exactly the same shape as the drop that entered the solution.

Precipitate

EQUATION: Producing copper hydroxide

Copper sulfate + sodium hydroxide ➪ copper hydroxide + sodium sulfate

$$CuSO_4(aq) + 2NaOH(aq) \; ➪ \; Cu(OH)_2(s) + Na_2SO_4(aq)$$
precipitate

◀ Gelatinous light blue copper hydroxide is changed to a soluble, very dark blue copper compound when concentrated ammonia solution is added.

2⁺

Copper

Nitrogen

Oxygen

Hydrogen

▶ A representation of the structure of the copper complex that is formed when excess ammonia solution is added to copper hydroxide.

Silver

Silver lies between copper and gold as one of the softest metals. It is the best conductor of heat and electricity of all the metals, but its softness and relative rarity mean that it has not been put into widespread use.

Silver, gold, platinum and mercury make up the noble metals. They share the common property that they do not oxidize readily when heated, and they will not dissolve in most mineral acids. Silver has been treasured since ancient times, and it is called a precious metal, as are gold, platinum, iridium and palladium.

The main use of silver in the past has been for coins and jewelry. Even here softness is a problem, and silver jewelry and coins are actually alloys of silver and copper. In fact, silver coins are at least one-tenth copper.

▼ Silver coins have been in existence for thousands of years. This is an example of a Greek tetradrachma showing Apollo. It was minted between 261 and 246 B.C.

▲ A silver Djambia scabbard from Yemen on the Arabian Peninsula. The silver denotes wealth and importance.

Sterling silver

Silver jewelry, cutlery and serving dishes are made of sterling silver. It consists of 92.5% silver and 7.5% copper, the copper being used to make the silver harder and more able to withstand the occasional blow without denting.

The reactivity of silver

Metals can be arranged in a list called the reactivity series, with the most reactive at the top and the least reactive at the bottom.

Silver is near the bottom of the reactivity series because it is only very slightly reactive. This low reactivity means that silver compounds are rarely produced in nature, and silver has very limited uses in chemistry. It will not react with the air to form oxides, although it does react with polluted air to form silver sulfide. This is, in fact, the chemical composition of the tarnishing seen on silver jewelry, cutlery and decorative ware, as described below.

alloy: a mixture of a metal and various other elements.

noble metals: silver, gold, platinum and mercury. These are the least reactive metals.

precious metal: silver, gold, platinum, iridium and palladium. Each is prized for its rarity. This category is the equivalent of gemstones for minerals.

reactivity: the tendency of a substance to react with other substances. The term is most widely used in comparing the reactivity of metals. Metals are arranged in a reactivity series.

REACTIVITY SERIES	
Element	*Reactivity*
potassium	*most reactive*
sodium	
calcium	
magnesium	
aluminum	
manganese	
chromium	
zinc	
iron	
cadmium	
tin	
lead	
copper	
mercury	
silver	
gold	
platinum	*least reactive*

▼ Silver metal reacts with hydrogen sulfide gas in the air to produce black silver sulfide.

Tarnish

Tarnish is the dark brown or black film that develops slowly on silverware, especially in industrial cities. Silver does not react with oxygen, so tarnish is not an oxide coating. Rather, it is a reaction of the silver with hydrogen sulfide in the air, especially the air near industrial cities. The result is a black film of silver sulfide as shown on the fork above and to the right.

Some silver tableware can tarnish (for example, the ends of forks) because some foods contain hydrogen sulfide. Hard boiled eggs are an example. The hydrogen sulfide effect can also be seen in the dark ring around the yolk.

EQUATION: Tarnishing of silver

Silver + hydrogen sulfide + oxygen ⇨ silver sulfide + water

$4Ag(s) + 2H_2S(g) + O_2(g) \Rightarrow 2Ag_2S(s) + 2H_2O(l)$

Silver and silver ores

Silver is a rare element, being 68th in the elements of the earth's crust. Because it reacts poorly, it is sometimes found as native (pure) silver metal. This allowed the Egyptians, for example, to use silver nearly 5,000 years ago. Similar native deposits, called lodes, have been found in the Americas. This attracted Spanish colonists in the 17th and 18th centuries, and the discovery of the Comstock Lode in Nevada in the 19th century caused a silver rush.

Outside these rare native deposits, silver is more commonly found as silver sulfide. Much silver is also found associated with other metals such as zinc and copper, and is recovered as a byproduct of refining these more plentiful metals.

Hydrothermal veins and native deposits

Native metals are found only in places that were once so hot that the metals existed in molten form. It is quite common to find deposits of all of the coinage metals together. This is because they are all products of hot liquids created during intense volcanic activity.

Deep below volcanoes lie their source chambers, full of liquid rock (called magma) that has forced its way up from deep within the Earth's crust. At the end of the volcanic activity, the magma chambers begin to cool, and many of the constituents crystallize out. At the same time, hot acidic liquids are produced that flow out from the magma into fissures in the surrounding rock. Here the hot solutions cool, and the various dissolved compounds solidify in fissures called veins.

Veins contain a variety of minerals, including metal compounds and native metals. These are the rich "lodes" that prospectors have sought through the centuries.

Less concentrated deposits have been produced by sedimentary processes, and the ores, though much more extensive, are far less rich in metal.

Layers of sedimentary rocks are pushed up by the rising magma.

Hydrothermal veins in which minerals are concentrated.

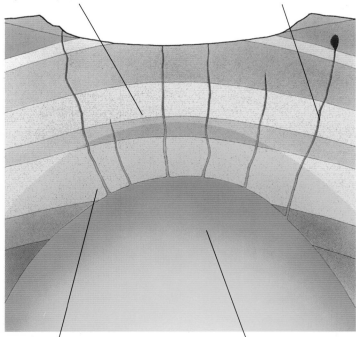

◀ This diagram shows how hydrothermal veins are related to the magma source, which subsequently cools to granite rock. Erosion often strips the surface rocks away, leaving deposits in a ring pattern around the granite.

Rocks around the hot magma chamber are metamorphosed, or changed.

Magma from below the Earth's crust initially heats the surrounding rocks but eventually cools to form granite.

Extraction and refining

Silver is present in small concentrations along with several other metals, such as copper, lead and zinc and it is usually extracted while these metals are being refined.

During electrical refining of copper, for example, the silver settles out at the bottom of the tank in which copper is being refined by electrolysis. The silver is dissolved out of the residue using concentrated nitric acid. The solution is then reacted with iron sulfate, and the silver comes out of solution as a precipitate. It is then further refined by electrolysis.

Silver also dissolves in solutions of sodium or potassium cyanide, and these substances can be used for chemical extraction. The reaction produces a solution containing silver cyanide to which zinc is added causing the silver metal to precipitate out. This method was developed just in time to be used to extract silver from the Comstock Lode.

Because cyanide is so dangerous, the cyanide process is little used today. Instead, a flotation process is used (see page 10). Jets of water create bubbles in tanks of ore powder containing a frothing agent. The silver is taken way in the froth and is then refined by electrical means.

Because so much silver is used in film-making, attempts are made to recover the silver on the film and recycle it during film processing. About one fifth of the silver used in film-making is recovered. This is done by burning the film and then refining the silver by electrical means.

gangue: the unwanted material in an ore.

hydrothermal: a process in which hot water is involved. It is usually used in the context of rock formation because hot water and other fluids sent outward from liquid magmas are important carriers of metals and the minerals that form gemstones.

lode: a number of veins of a metal found close together.

ore: a rock containing enough of a useful substance to make mining it worthwhile.

vein: a mineral deposit different from, and usually cutting across, the surrounding rocks. Most mineral and metal-bearing veins are deposits filling fractures. The veins were filled by hot, mineral-rich waters rising upward from liquid volcanic magma. They are important sources of many metals, such as silver and gold, and also minerals such as gemstones. Veins are usually narrow and were best suited to hand-mining. They are less exploited in the modern machine age.

EQUATION: The use of cyanide to extract silver

Silver cyanide complex + zinc ⇨ zinc cyanide complex + silver

$$2NaAg(CN)_2(aq) \quad + \quad Zn(s) \quad ⇨ \quad Na_2Zn(CN)_4(aq) \quad + \quad 2Ag(s)$$

Also...

The Comstock Lode was a zone nearly six kilometers long that included deposits of native silver. It was discovered in the Sierra Nevada mountains of Nevada, in 1859. It was named after the prospector who found the lode, Henry T. P. Comstock.

The area produced one of the richest silver rushes in history, probably yielding some $300 million at 19th century values (many billions in today's values). Virginia City was founded and grew up around the lode. When the silver was mined out, people moved away, and Virginia City is now a ghost town.

◄ The wealth of the town of Taxco in central Mexico was based on a silver lode discovered nearby. The lode is still worked, although most of the native metal has been removed in the past two centuries. The grand church and other buildings reflect the money that the exploitation of silver brought to this otherwise poor rural area.

Silver in photography

Because silver compounds are light-sensitive, about four-tenths of all the silver used industrially goes into making photographic film.

The film is made of a plastic base over which is spread a thin layer of gelatin that contains silver salt. This gelatin layer is known as the emulsion layer.

Various silver salts are used in the emulsion. Silver iodide reacts fastest to light, and is used for fast-speed films. Silver bromide is slightly less sensitive, and is used for slower speeds. Silver bromide and silver chloride are light-sensitive chemicals that are placed on the surface of developing papers.

How light-sensitive silver salts work

Silver salts become reduced upon exposure to light. This converts parts of the salts to silver metal.

When the film is placed in the developer, another chemical reaction takes place in which the silver salts are further reduced. Those that were not affected by light are reduced more slowly, leaving some areas darker than others.

The developed film is placed in a "fixing" solution to stop the process after it has fully reacted with the silver salts that were exposed to light. The process leaves a negative image on the acetate film.

A print is made by shining light through the negative onto photographic paper that has a coating containing silver chloride crystals. This material has to be developed and fixed in the same way as the film. At the end of the process a positive print is obtained.

▼▼ These two test tubes show the effect of light on some silver compounds. The test tube above shows a precipitate of silver chloride the instant after it was produced. The one below shows the change that has occurred within one minute. The way that silver salts darken on exposure to light is the basis of the photographic process.

◄ A film negative containing stabilized silver (the dark part) within the gelatin. Although it is no longer light-sensitive, it still has a gelatin layer and so is liable to be scratched if handled carelessly. The clear areas are the places where no light reached the film. The silver salts have been washed away from these areas.

▲ A positive print from the last century. The yellow coloring on this print results from the same process as the tarnishing described on page 29. The hydrogen sulfide gas present in the air reacts with the silver in the print, darkening it.

halide: a salt of one of the halogens (fluorine, chlorine, bromine and iodine).

oxidation/reduction: a reaction in which oxygen is gained or lost, respectively.

Also...

Silver is not attacked by most acids. However, it does react with concentrated nitric acid, liberating brown nitrogen dioxide gas and forming a solution of silver nitrate. This solution will precipitate halides. Silver chloride is a white solid, that quickly darkens in sunlight; silver bromide is a pale yellow solid and silver iodide is a dark yellow solid. All three of these solids disappear into a colorless solution if sodium thiosulfate solution (hypo) is added. This is why "hypo-fixer" works, since this solution can be washed off the film or photographic print paper.

▲ Sodium thiosulfate

EQUATION: Silver bromide and photographers' hypo

Sodium thiosulfate (photographers' hypo) + silver bromide ⇨ silver complex + sodium bromide

$$2Na_2S_2O_3(aq) \quad + \quad AgBr(s) \quad ⇨ \quad Na_3Ag(S_2O_3)_2(aq) \quad + \quad NaBr(aq)$$

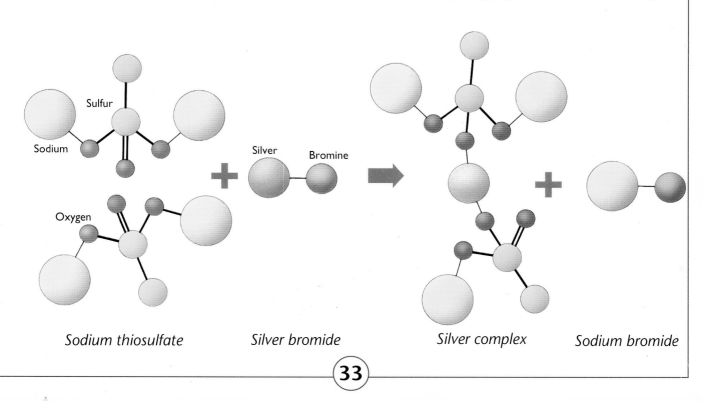

Sodium thiosulfate   Silver bromide   Silver complex   Sodium bromide

Everyday uses of silver

One of the most common objects around the home is the mirror. Mirrors reflect light rays to form an image.

The earliest form of mirror was a disk of polished bronze. However, although this gave some kind of image, the poor reflecting properties of bronze, and the fact that it tarnishes quickly, were serious drawbacks.

The next improvement, and in common use in the Middle Ages, was to use sheets of glass with metal foil attached to the back. Silver was the preferred metal for this because it was soft and could be beaten into thin sheets, and because it is highly reflective.

However, silver tarnishes over time in polluted air (the surface develops a dark silver sulfide coat). To produce a durable mirror, it was necessary to combine the strength of glass and the reflecting properties of silver by binding the silver to the glass so that hydrogen sulfide in the polluted air could not tarnish the surface.

In 1835 Justus von Liebig developed a way of depositing silver onto glass. The method, known as silvering, is still in use today.

Making a mirror in a tube

To make a mirror in a test tube, silver nitrate, silver hydroxide and ammonia are mixed together in solution together with a reducing agent, in this case glucose.
The tube is then placed in a bath of hot water. Silver is precipitated onto the warm glass tube.

▶ A silvered mirror produced on the inside of a test tube.

High-quality mirrors

Specialized mirrors are need for precision scientific work. For these, silver is vaporized by heating it in a vacuum chamber. It is then condensed onto the glass as a thin, even coating.

For a large-scale use of mirrors, such as in solar power stations, aluminum is often used as a substitute for silver. It is not quite so good a reflector, but it is very much cheaper.

amalgam: a liquid alloy of mercury with another metal.

cell: a vessel containing two electrodes and an electrolyte.

electrolyte: a solution that conducts electricity.

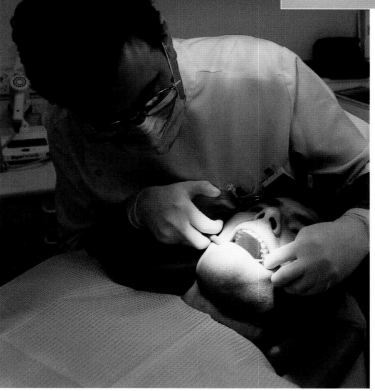

◄▲ The metal-based fillings in grinding teeth are made with either silver or gold amalgams.

In silver-based amalgam the proportions of metals by weight are: 52% mercury, 33% silver, 12.5% tin, 2% copper and 0.5% zinc.

As the amalgam sets, it expands slightly, locking itself into the tooth cavity.

Also...

If you have metal-based amalgam fillings and you chew a piece of "silver" or other metal foil, it is possible to get a shooting sensation through the filled teeth. In effect you will be repeating one of the world's earliest electrical experiments, in which Luigi Galvani made frogs' legs twitch by using the body fluids and two different metals to create a battery (an electrical cell). In the case of the silver foil, the amalgam and the silver foil are two different metal electrodes, and your saliva is the electrolyte of the cell, so that a current flows. This current may well cause a painful sensation in your tooth if the filled cavity is deep and the filling is close to the dental nerve.

Gold in the Earth

Gold mostly forms in veins in rocks. The source of gold is probably hot liquids that boiled off the great molten bodies that feed volcanoes. These hot fluids forced their way up through the cracks in the overlying rocks, where they cooled and solidified.

Gold is among a number of metals (including silver, copper and tin) that form in this way. Scientists call the veins hydrothermal (hot water) deposits.

Gold is so unreactive chemically that it does not easily form oxides or other compounds and remains as "native" (pure) metal in the rocks.

Mining

Vein, or lode, mining is the most important of all gold recovery methods (see page 30). Although each ounce of gold recovered requires about 100,000 ounces of ore to be processed, so much gold is deposited in rock veins that this method accounts for more than half of the world's total gold production today. The gold in the veins may be microscopic particles, nuggets, sheets, or gold compounds. Regardless of how it is found, the ore requires extensive extraction and refining.

◀ A vein carrying gold in a mine tunnel.

▼ A modern open-pit gold mine near Bendigo, Australia.

hydrothermal: a process in which hot water is involved. It is usually used in the context of rock formation because hot water and other fluids sent outward from liquid magmas are important carriers of metals and the minerals that form gemstones.

lode: a number of veins of a metal found close together.

vein: a mineral deposit different from, and usually cutting across, the surrounding rocks. Most mineral and metal-bearing veins are deposits filling fractures. The veins were filled by hot, mineral-rich waters rising upward from liquid volcanic magma. They are important sources of many metals, such as silver and gold, and also minerals such as gemstones. Veins are usually narrow and were best suited to hand-mining. They are less exploited in the modern machine age.

▲ A gold nugget and flakes. Each flake is about 3 mm long.

◄ The largest piece of native gold ever found. Pieces of gold like this are called gold nuggets. This one, called Perseverance, was found in the South African province of Natal on December 16, 1874. It weighed 3.3 kg and was just over 12 cm long.

▼ Early 20th-century mining had become big business, rather than the province of many small-scale prospectors working by hand.

Gold rushes

Because people have put such a high value on gold, its presence has attracted much attention throughout the ages. One of the main reasons for Spanish and Portuguese explorers taking an interest in South America was to plunder them as a source of gold.

The 19th century saw several major gold rushes in the United States, Canada, Russia, South Africa and Australia. The 1848–49 gold rush in California produced more new gold than had been found in the previous three centuries and made the United States the largest gold producer in the world. But as these gold fields were worked out, others took their place in Alaska, Australia (particularly Victoria) and South Africa (The Transvaal). Of the probable gold reserves, about half are to be found in the Witwatersrand area of South Africa.

Gold at the surface

Much of the gold found during a gold rush was collected from river beds rather than from veins of gold dug from mines. Gold occurs in river beds as a result of natural landscape erosion. Where the gold veins are exposed at the land surface, erosion eventually breaks them down into small fragments and carries them away in streams and rivers.

However, because gold is such a heavy element, it is not easily moved and so it accumulates in river beds. The fragments of gold are very small, but they are not found among the tiny fragments of other kinds of rock. Rather, they settle out among gravels and larger pieces of rock. This is because sand and pebbles are made of silica, a mineral that is much less dense than gold. A fast-flowing stream will carry small, but denser, particles of heavy gold along with larger but less dense gravel.

Sluice boxes and dredging

The sluice box, shown below, is a much more efficient way of collecting gold. The larger pebbles are screened away and the other fragments washed down a chute. Bars placed along the chute collect the heavy gold, while the rest is washed away. Washing river sediment over wool fleeces is another way to collect gold.

Most placer deposits, especially those worked in navigable rivers and in coastal areas, are now mined on a far larger scale using dredges.

▼ A man using a sluice box in Canada at the turn of the century

Panning

The accumulation of gold in river sediments is known as a placer deposit. The gold can be separated by hand in a method known as gold panning. Because it is heavy, gold resists being washed away. The gold particles can be separated from sand by swirling the pan around in a little water. The gold will remain in the center of the pan while the sand swirls off the edges.

◀ Panning gold in a river in Alaska

Amalgamation: using mercury to refine gold

Another way to recover gold from placer deposits is by making the gold into a liquid alloy with mercury, known as an amalgam.

In this age-old process the mercury and gold-containing sediment are heated, causing the gold to amalgamate with the mercury. The amalgam can then be drawn off and dissolved in dilute sodium cyanide. When zinc is added to the solution, gold is precipitated to the bottom of the vessel.

Amalgamation recovers about two-thirds of the gold in an ore. To extract the remainder, other chemical methods have to be used.

This process uses a range of highly poisonous substances and has to be carried out in carefully controlled conditions. Nevertheless, despite the risks, refining using mercury is done on a small scale by prospectors, for example, in the depths of the Brazilian rainforest. The waste products of this process are flushed into the rivers, where they pollute whole stretches of river water that are used as drinking supplies.

Many of the prospectors breathe in the mercury vapor as the amalgam is heated, causing long-term (and even fatal) damage to their health.

Chemical refining

Chemical refining is the last stage of the refining process. It can be applied to gold sediment that has already been partly refined using amalgamation or to the sludge produced in copper and zinc refining.

Like silver, gold can be dissolved in sodium cyanide. When metallic zinc is added to the solution, the gold is precipitated.

EQUATION: Precipitation of gold using sodium cyanide and zinc

Sodium cyanide + gold amalgam + water + oxygen ⇨ *cyanide complex + sodium hydroxide*

$$8NaCN(s) + 4Au(s) + 2H_2O(l) + O_2(g) \Rightarrow 4NaAu(CN)_2(aq) + 4NaOH(aq)$$

Cyanide complex + zinc ⇨ *cyanide complex + gold*

$$2NaAu(CN)_2(aq) + Zn(s) \Rightarrow Na_2Zn(CN)_4(aq) + 2Au(s)$$

Uses of gold

Gold is the most easily worked of all metals. This means that it can be drawn out into fine wires or beaten into sheets so thin that they are almost transparent. At this stage the gold is just a few atoms thick.

One of the most common uses of thin sheets of gold is as gold leaf, a decorative material that is used on furniture, walls and religious objects. Many people use gold leaf as part of their religious devotions. Gold has also played an important part in the world's money supply (see next page).

Carat

The purity of gold is measured in carats. Pure gold is known as 24 carat gold. Other forms of gold are alloys of gold with silver, copper or nickel.

The carat number shows how much gold is in each alloy. Thus 8 carat gold contains $^8/_{24}$ths or one-third gold; 18 carat gold contains $^{18}/_{24}$ths or three-quarters gold and so on. White gold has the lowest concentration of gold, being $^6/_{24}$ths gold and one-quarter nickel.

▲ Gold has been used decoratively since the earliest times both for jewelry and decorative ware, and for adornment to buildings (as in St. Mark's cathedral, Venice, shown here). Gold retains its shine even when used outdoors, which is why gold leaf is used on the domes of some buildings.

▼ Gold leaf being used in a Buddhist ceremony.

The reactivity of gold

Gold is near the bottom of the reactivity series because it almost unreactive. Gold will not react with the air to form oxides. Traditionally only a mixture of concentrated nitric acid and concentrated hydrochloric acid (called *aqua regia*) would dissolve gold.

REACTIVITY SERIES	
Element	Reactivity
potassium	most reactive
sodium	
calcium	
magnesium	
aluminum	
manganese	
chromium	
zinc	
iron	
cadmium	
tin	
lead	
copper	
mercury	
silver	
gold	
platinum	least reactive

electrolysis: an electrical-chemical process that uses an electric current to cause the breakup of a compound and the movement of metal ions in a solution. The process happens in many natural situations (as for example in rusting) and is also commonly used in industry for purifying (refining) metals or for plating metal objects with a fine, even metal coating.

ion: an atom, or group of atoms, that has gained or lost one or more electrons and so developed an electrical charge

reactivity: the tendency of a substance to react with other substances. The term is most widely used in comparing the reactivity of metals. Metals are arranged in a reactivity series.

Gold and coinage

The first use of metal as a form of currency goes back to the ancient Egyptians about six thousand years ago. Gold, silver and copper were most often used, hence their grouping into the coinage metals. The metals were poured into molds to produce blank discs called planchets. Markings were stamped on their faces by pressing them between two bronze dies. The coins usually had their value on one side and the head of the ruler on the other as a guarantee.

Gold will not stand up to handling unless it is alloyed with other metals. For example, in the United States gold coins (made until 1933) were 90% gold and the remainder silver and copper.

Gold was once used as a worldwide currency reserve, and was held in vaults as a guarantee of the paper money in circulation. This system no longer operates, and gold can be bought and sold on the open market. However, it is still true that when people feel nervous about a currency, they buy gold, thus forcing up gold prices.

There are still large reserves of gold, the largest being at Fort Knox, Kentucky, which contains both bullion (bars) and coins.

▼ A Krugerrand, one of the world's most famous gold coins.

Gold alloys and gold plating

Gold is not only rare, it is a very soft metal. For many reasons it is sensible to alloy it with other metals to improve its characteristics for use.

Gold is most often alloyed with copper and silver. This changes the strength and color of the alloy as well as making the gold go farther. The resulting alloys are cheaper than pure gold.

"Green gold" is an alloy of gold, silver and copper with silver in the greatest proportion. In "red gold" copper dominates the alloy, and an alloy of gold and nickel is called "white gold."

Gold can be formed into alloys with mercury called amalgams; these are often used as dental fillings. Gold can also be plated onto objects to increase their resistance to corrosion.

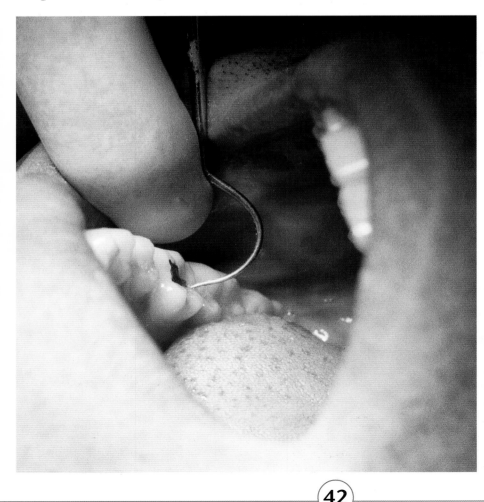

▲ The brooch shown here is a real orchid that has been coated in gold using electrolysis. The orchid was dipped in a resin, and the edges of the petals painted with a metal paint so that it could be made into an electrical conductor. Then it was suspended in a bath of electrolyte. As an electric current flowed, the gold was deposited onto the metal-coated flower.

◄ A gold filling in a lower tooth. In some countries gold fillings are a sign of wealth. Gold is a suitable material for a filling because it will amalgamate with mercury and then not react with body fluids, neither releasing toxic substances nor being corroded by the body.

The metal-based fillings in grinding teeth are made with either silver or gold amalgams. Gold fillings contain gold alloyed with palladium and copper. Rhodium is often added as a hardener for the gold-palladium alloy. Gold instead of silver is also often used in places where the filling is more liable to show, such as in holes in the front teeth.

Using gold in industry

Gold is almost entirely nonreactive. Although this means that gold will not form compounds, it also means that, where nonreactive materials are needed, gold has an important part to play. Because it is rare, it is also expensive to use. This is why gold is used only where such materials are important.

Gold is a good conductor of electricity and does not oxidize, so it is important for use in electrical circuits, such as micro-electronics, and for connectors and switches. Most of the gold used is electroplated onto some less expensive base material.

Also, because it is doesn't corrode, gold is used in places where there are corrosive atmospheres, such as in certain chemical processes. For the same reason, gold can be used safely in amalgams to make dental fillings.

Gold can also have an important role in tiny amounts. For example, it is used in glass to produce a heat shield.

alloy: a mixture of a metal and various other elements.

electrolysis: an electrical-chemical process that uses an electric current to cause the breakup of a compound and the movement of metal ions in a solution. The process happens in many natural situations (as for example in rusting) and is also commonly used in industry for purifying (refining) metals or for plating metal objects with a fine, even metal coating.

electrolyte: a solution that conducts electricity.

electroplating: depositing a thin layer of a metal onto the surface of another substance using electrolysis.

Gold plating

Gold can be deposited as a fine layer on the surface of many materials. Usually it is applied by electrolysis after being dissolved in a cyanide solution. The thickness of gold plate obtained this way can be as little as two-millionths of a centimeter.

Some metals become coated with gold automatically if they are dipped in a gold cyanide solution, because a natural battery is established between the gold and the metal. Gold can be deposited onto nickel in this way.

◄ Gold does not oxidize, so no insulating oxide layer builds up on its surface (as happens, for example, with aluminum). This is the reason gold-plated contacts are used in many electrical circuits where it is important that good long-term contact is made. This is a terminator from a computer.

Key facts about...

Copper

A soft, orangy-red metal, chemical symbol Cu

Forms alloys with other metals easily

Turns green when exposed to the air

Essential for plant growth

Good conductor of electricity

Scarce metal, making only 70 parts per million of the Earth's crust

Good conductor of heat

Has no taste

Has no smell

Melts at 1,083°C, a lower temperature than many other metals

Atomic number 29, atomic weight about 64

Silver

A soft, white metal, chemical symbol Ag

Forms alloys with copper to give it additional strength

Turns brown slowly (tarnishes) when exposed to polluted air

Scarce metal, making only one hundred-millionth of the Earth's crust

The best conductor of electricity of any metal

The best conductor of heat of any metal

Has no taste

Has no smell

Soft and easily worked

Best natural reflector of light

Melts at 960°C

Atomic number 47, atomic weight about 108

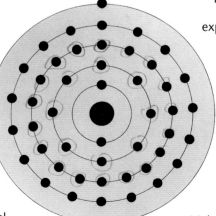

Gold

A soft, yellow metal, chemical symbol Au

Does not tarnish in air

Will not react with acids

Good conductor of electricity

Scarce metal, making only 4 parts per hundred million of the Earth's crust

Good conductor of heat

Has no taste

Can be worked into extremely thin sheets or fine wires

Has no smell

Melts at 1,063°C

Atomic number 79, atomic weight about 197

◄▼ These two pictures show the two sides of a Roman silver denarius, minted in 77 B.C. The side shown on the left shows the helmeted Roma, allegory of the city of Rome, and the side shown below portrays the she-wolf, which refers to the founding of Rome by Romulus and Remus, mythical twins who were adopted and raised in infancy by a wolf.

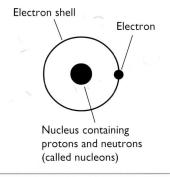

SHELL DIAGRAMS

The shell diagrams on these two pages are representations of an atom of each element. The total number of electrons is shown in the relevant orbitals, or shells, around the central nucleus.

Electron shell

Electron

Nucleus containing protons and neutrons (called nucleons)

The Periodic Table

The Periodic Table sets out the relationships among the elements of the Universe. According to the Periodic Table, certain elements fall into groups. The pattern of these groups has, in the past, allowed scientists to predict elements that had not at that time been discovered. It can still be used today to predict the properties of unfamiliar elements.

The Periodic Table was first described by a Russian teacher, Dmitry Ivanovich Mendeleev, between 1869 and 1870. He was interested in writing a chemistry textbook and wanted to show his students that there were certain patterns in the elements that had been discovered. So he set out the elements (of which there were 57 at the time) according to their known properties. On the assumption that there was pattern to the elements, he left blank spaces where elements seemed to be missing. Using this first version of the Periodic Table, he was able to predict in detail the chemical and physical properties of elements that had not yet been discovered. Other scientists began to look for the missing elements, and they soon found them.

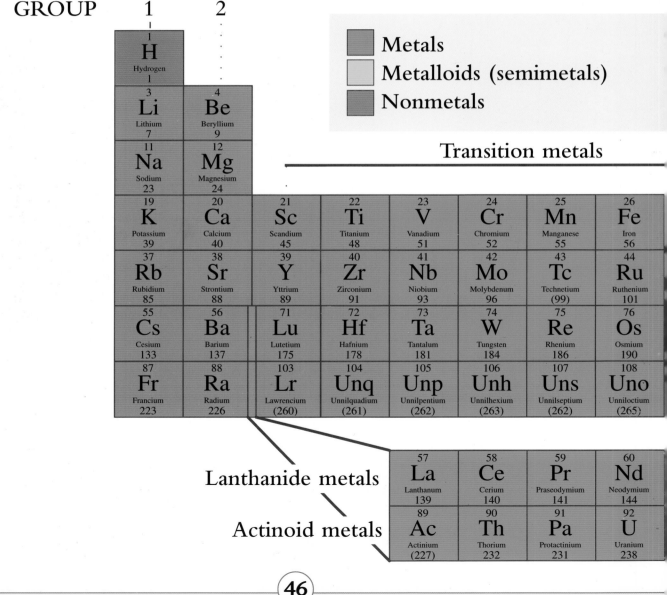

GROUP

Metals
Metalloids (semimetals)
Nonmetals

Transition metals

Lanthanide metals

Actinoid metals

Hydrogen did not seem to fit into the table, and so he placed it in a box on its own. Otherwise the elements were all placed horizontally. When an element was reached with properties similar to the first one in the top row, a second row was started. By following this rule, similarities among the elements can be found by reading up and down. By reading across the rows, the elements progressively increase their atomic number. This number indicates the number of positively charged particles (protons) in the nucleus of each atom. This is also the number of negatively charged particles (electrons) in the atom.

The chemical properties of an element depend on the number of electrons in the outermost shell.

Atoms can form compounds by sharing electrons in their outermost shells. This explains why atoms with a full set of electrons (like helium, an inert gas) are unreactive, whereas atoms with an incomplete electron shell (such as chlorine) are very reactive. Elements can also combine by the complete transfer of electrons from metals to nonmetals, and the compounds formed contain ions.

Radioactive elements lose particles from their nucleus and electrons from their surrounding shells. As a result they change their atomic number and so become new elements.

Atomic (proton) number

13 — Symbol
Al
Aluminum
27 — Name

Approximate relative atomic mass

							3	4	5	6	7	0
												2 **He** Helium 4
							5 **B** Boron 11	6 **C** Carbon 12	7 **N** Nitrogen 14	8 **O** Oxygen 16	9 **F** Fluorine 19	10 **Ne** Neon 20
							13 **Al** Aluminum 27	14 **Si** Silicon 28	15 **P** Phosphorus 31	16 **S** Sulfur 32	17 **Cl** Chlorine 35	18 **Ar** Argon 40
27 **Co** Cobalt 59	28 **Ni** Nickel 59	29 **Cu** Copper 64	30 **Zn** Zinc 65	31 **Ga** Gallium 70	32 **Ge** Germanium 73	33 **As** Arsenic 75	34 **Se** Selenium 79	35 **Br** Bromine 80	36 **Kr** Krypton 84
45 **Rh** Rhodium 103	46 **Pd** Palladium 106	47 **Ag** Silver 108	48 **Cd** Cadmium 112	49 **In** Indium 115	50 **Sn** Tin 119	51 **Sb** Antimony 122	52 **Te** Tellurium 128	53 **I** Iodine 127	54 **Xe** Xenon 131
77 **Ir** Iridium 192	78 **Pt** Platinum 195	79 **Au** Gold 197	80 **Hg** Mercury 201	81 **Tl** Thallium 204	82 **Pb** Lead 207	83 **Bi** Bismuth 209	84 **Po** Polonium (209)	85 **At** Astatine (210)	86 **Rn** Radon (222)
109 **Une** Unnilennium (266)									

61 **Pm** Promethium (145)	62 **Sm** Samarium 150	63 **Eu** Europium 152	64 **Gd** Gadolinium 157	65 **Tb** Terbium 159	66 **Dy** Dysprosium 163	67 **Ho** Holmium 165	68 **Er** Erbium 167	69 **Tm** Thulium 169	70 **Yb** Ytterbium 173
93 **Np** Neptunium (237)	94 **Pu** Plutonium (244)	95 **Am** Americium (243)	96 **Cm** Curium (247)	97 **Bk** Berkelium (247)	98 **Cf** Californium (251)	99 **Es** Einsteinium (252)	100 **Fm** Fermium (257)	101 **Md** Mendelevium (258)	102 **No** Nobelium (259)

Understanding equations

As you read through this book, you will notice that many pages contain equations using symbols. If you are not familiar with these symbols, read this page. Symbols make it easy for chemists to write out the reactions that are occurring in a way that allows a better understanding of the processes involved.

Symbols for the elements

The basis of the modern use of symbols for elements dates back to the 19th century. At this time a shorthand was developed using the first letter of the element wherever possible. Thus "O" stands for oxygen, "H" stands for hydrogen

and so on. However, if we were to use only the first letter, then there could be some confusion. For example, nitrogen and nickel would both use the symbols N. To overcome this problem, many elements are symbolized using the first two letters of their full name, and the second letter is not in capitals. Thus although nitrogen is N, nickel becomes Ni. Not all symbols come from the English name; many use the Latin name instead. This is why, for example, gold is not G but Au (for the Latin *aurum*) and sodium has the symbol Na, from the Latin *natrium*.

Compounds of elements are made by combining letters. Thus the molecule carbon

Written and symbolic equations

In this book important chemical equations are briefly stated in words (these are called word equations) and are then shown in their symbolic form along with the states.

What reaction the equation illustrates

Written equation

Symbol equation

EQUATION: The formation of calcium hydroxide

Calcium oxide + water ⇨ calcium hydroxide

$$CaO(s) \quad + \quad H_2O(l) \quad \Rightarrow \quad Ca(OH)_2(aq)$$

heated

Sometimes you will find an additional description below the symbolic equation.

Symbol showing the state:
s is for solid, l is for liquid,
g is for gas and aq is for aqueous.

Diagrams

Some of the equations are shown as graphic representations.

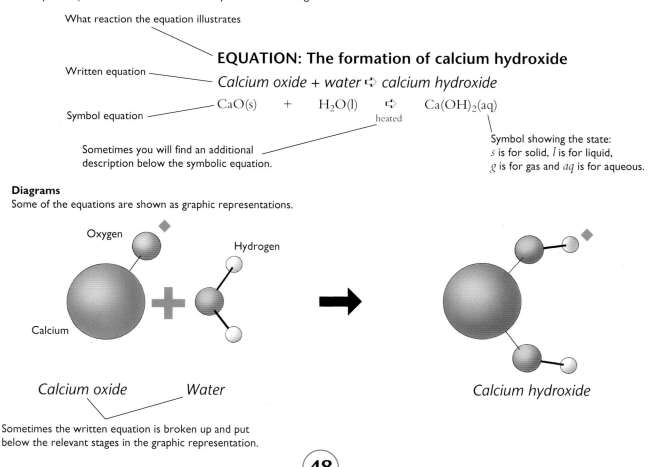

Oxygen

Hydrogen

Calcium

Calcium oxide   *Water*

Calcium hydroxide

Sometimes the written equation is broken up and put below the relevant stages in the graphic representation.

monoxide is CO. By using letters that are not capitals for the second letter of an element, it is possible to show that cobalt, symbol Co, is not the same as the molecule carbon monoxide, CO.

However, the letters can be made to do much more than this. In many molecules, atoms combine in unequal numbers. So, for example, carbon dioxide has one atom of carbon for every two of oxygen. This is shown by using the number 2 beside the oxygen, and the symbol becomes CO_2.

In practice, some groups of atoms combine as a unit with other substances. Thus, for example, calcium bicarbonate (one of the compounds used in some antacid pills) is written $Ca(HCO_3)_2$. This shows that the part of the substance inside the brackets reacts as a unit, and the "2" outside the brackets shows the presence of two such units.

Some substances attract water molecules to themselves. To show this a dot is used. Thus the blue-colored form of copper sulfate is written $CuSO_4.5H_2O$. In this case five molecules of water attract to one copper sulfate. When you see the dot, you know that this water can be driven off by heating; it is part of the crystal structure.

In a reaction substances change by rearranging the combinations of atoms. The way they change is shown by using the chemical symbols, placing those that will react (the starting materials, or reactants) on the left and the products of the reaction on the right. Between the two, chemists use an arrow to show which way the reaction is occurring.

It is possible to describe a reaction in words. This gives a word equation. Word equations are used throughout this book. However, it is easier to understand what is happening by using an equation containing symbols. These are also given in many places. They are not used when the equations are very complex.

In any equation both sides balance; that is, there must be an equal number of like atoms on both sides of the arrow. When you try to write down reactions, you, too, must balance your equation; you cannot have a few atoms left over at the end!

The symbols in brackets are abbreviations for the physical state of each substance taking part, so that (s) is used for solid, (l) for liquid, (g) for gas and (aq) for an aqueous solution, that is, a solution of a substance dissolved in water.

Atoms and ions
Each sphere represents a particle of an element. A particle can be an atom or an ion. Each atom or ion is associated with other atoms or ions through bonds – forces of attraction. The size of the particles and the nature of the bonds can be extremely important in determining the nature of the reaction or the properties of the compound.

Chemical symbols, equations and diagrams
The arrangement of any molecule or compound can be shown in one of the two ways below, depending on which gives the clearer picture. The left-hand diagram is called a ball-and-stick diagram because it uses rods and spheres to show the structure of the material. This example shows water, H_2O. There are two hydrogen atoms and one oxygen atom.

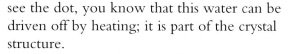

Sodium

This indicates that the compound is ionic.

▶ This represents a unit of sodium bicarbonate ($NaHCO_3$).

The term "unit" is sometimes used to simplify the representation of a combination of ions.

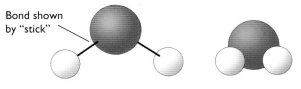

Bond shown by "stick"

Colors too
The colors of each of the particles help differentiate the elements involved. The diagram can then be matched to the written and symbolic equation given with the diagram. In the case above, oxygen is red and hydrogen is gray.

Glossary of technical terms

alloy: a mixture of a metal and various other elements.

amalgam: a liquid alloy of mercury with another metal.

anhydrous: a term meaning that water has been removed by heating. Many hydrated salts are crystalline. When they are heated and the water is driven off, the material changes to an anhydrous powder.

brazing: a form of soldering in which brass is used as the joining metal.

cell: a vessel containing two electrodes and an electrolyte that can act as an electrical conductor.

corrosion: the *slow* decay of a substance resulting from contact with gases and liquids in the environment. The term is often applied to metals. Rust is the corrosion of iron.

electrolysis: an electrical-chemical process that uses an electric current to cause the breakup of a compound and the movement of metal ions in a solution. The process happens in many natural situations (as for example in rusting) and is also commonly used in industry for purifying (refining) metals or for plating metal objects with a fine, even metal coating.

electrolyte: a solution that conducts electricity.

electron: a tiny, negatively charged particle that is part of an atom. The flow of electrons through a solid material such as a wire produces an electric current.

electroplating: depositing a thin layer of a metal onto the surface of another substance using electrolysis.

gangue: the unwanted material in an ore.

gelatinous: a term meaning made with water. Because a gelatinous precipitate is mostly water, it is of a similar density to water and will float or lie suspended in the liquid.

halide: a salt of one of the halogens (fluorine, chlorine, bromine and iodine).

hydrate: a solid compound in crystalline form that contains molecular water. Hydrates commonly form when a solution of a soluble salt is evaporated.

The water that forms part of a hydrate crystal is known as the "water of crystallization." It can usually be removed by heating, leaving an anhydrous salt.

hydrothermal: a process in which hot water is involved. It is usually used in the context of rock formation because hot water and other fluids sent outward from liquid magmas are important carriers of metals and the minerals that form gemstones.

ion: an atom, or group of atoms, that has gained or lost one or more electrons and so developed an electrical charge. Ions behave differently from electrically neutral atoms and molecules. They can move in an electric field, and they can also bind strongly to solvent molecules such as water. Positively charged ions are called cations; negatively charged ions are called anions. Ions carry electrical current through solutions.

lode: a number of veins of a metal found close together.

magma: the molten rock that forms a balloon-shaped chamber in the rock below a volcano. It is fed by rock moving upward from below the crust.

micronutrient: an element that the body requires in small amounts. Another term is trace element.

native metal: a pure form of a metal, not combined as a compound. Native metal is more common in poorly reactive elements than in those that are very reactive.

noble metals: silver, gold, platinum and mercury. These are the least reactive metals.

ore: a rock containing enough of a useful substance to make mining it worthwhile.

oxidation/reduction: a reaction in which oxygen is gained or lost, respectively.

oxide: a compound that includes oxygen and one other element.

patina: a surface coating that develops on metals and protects them from further corrosion.

placer deposit: a kind of ore body made of a sediment that contains fragments of gold ore eroded from a mother lode and transported by rivers or ocean currents.

porous: a material containing many small holes or cracks. Quite often the pores are connected, and liquids, such as water or oil, can move through them.

precious metal: silver, gold, platinum, iridium and palladium. Each is prized for its rarity. This category is the equivalent of gemstones for minerals.

protein: molecules that help build tissue and bone and therefore make new body cells. Proteins contain amino acids.

reactivity: the tendency of a substance to react with other substances. The term is most widely used in comparing the reactivity of metals. Metals are arranged in a reactivity series.

reagent: a starting material for a reaction.

reduction: the removal of oxygen from a substance.

refining: the separation of a mixture into the simpler substances of which it is made. In the case of a rock, it means the extraction of the metal that is mixed up in the rock.

sediment: material that settles out at the bottom of a liquid when it is still.

silicate: a compound containing silicon and oxygen (known as silica).

slag: a mixture of substances that are waste products of a furnace. Most slags are composed mainly of silicates.

sulfide: a sulfur compound that contains no oxygen.

vein: a mineral deposit different from, and usually cutting across, the surrounding rocks. Most mineral and metal-bearing veins are deposits filling fractures. The veins were filled by hot, mineral-rich waters rising upward from liquid volcanic magma. They are important sources of many metals, such as silver and gold, and also minerals such as gemstones. Veins are usually narrow and were best suited to hand-mining. They are less exploited in the modern machine age.

Master Index